BABAR'S ABC

BABAR'S

Laurent de Brunhoff

ABC

Harry N. Abrams, Inc., Publishers

Aa

airport

Alexander aims his arrow at the apple.

Arthur plays an accordion.

B b
Babar

A **bear** reads a **book** in **bed**.

The **bird blows** out the candles on the **birthday** cake.

Cc
circus

The **cat climbs** onto the camel.

Celeste wears her **crown** when she drives her **car**.

The **crocodile
cannot catch** the **crow**.

Dd
dog

Sometimes a **doll** needs a **doctor**.

This **duck** beats a **drum**.

Ee
elephant

White rabbits have long pink **ears** and little pink **eyes**.

Ff
fire fighter

The **fox follows** the **footprints**.

A **frog** plays a **flute** in the **flower** garden.

Flora feeds the **fish**.

G g
giraffe

The **geese go** out the garden gate.

Hh
Halloween

A **hippopotamus** steps on a **hose**.

The **helicopter** blows off Celeste's **hat**.

Ii
ice skating

Do not touch the hot **iron**!

Oops! Arthur spills the **ink**.

Jj
jungle

Zephir gets **jam** on his **jacket** when he **juggles** the **jars**.

Kk
kitchen

The **kangaroo kicks** the ball to the **koala**.

Kittens love kisses.

L l
ladder

A **little lamb licks** Pom's **lollipop**.

The **lazy lion lies** on the **log**.

Mm
merry-go-round

The **magician** **makes** the **monkey** change into a **mouse**.

N n
nest

Hammering **nails** is **noisy**!

Cornelius **needs** a **net** to catch butterflies.

Oo
orchestra

This **ostrich** likes to eat **oranges**.

The **owl** and **opossum** . . .

sleep in the **oak** tree.

Babar has **oil** spots **on** his **overalls**.

BABAR

P p
playground

A **parrot perches** on a **palm** tree.

Pom paints a **picture** of a **peach**.

The **pretty peacock** is lost among the **penguins**.

This **pig** wears **purple**-striped **pajamas**.

Q q

queen

A **quilt** keeps the **queen** warm.

Rr
rhinoceros

Rabbits **really** like **radishes**.

This **reindeer** has a **red** nose.

S s
seashore

Squirrels do not like the smell of skunks.

Seals and sharks swim in the sea.

T t
tugboat

The tiger tells stories on television.

The turtle rides the tricycle.

U u
unicorn

Alexander and Babar keep dry **under** their **umbrellas**.

Vv
van

Ww
wagon

X x
x-ray

Y y
yak

Zz
zebra

Zephir zips up his sleeping bag **zipper**.

DESIGNER, ABRAMS EDITION: Darilyn Lowe Carnes

The artwork for each picture is prepared using watercolor on paper.
This text is set in 17-point Comic Sans.

Library of Congress Cataloging-in-Publication Data

Brunhoff, Laurent de.
    Babar's ABC / Laurent de Brunhoff.
        p. cm.
    ISBN 0-8109-5707-8
    [1. English language—Alphabet—Juvenile literature. 2. Babar
(Fictious character)—Juvenile literature. 3. Vocabulary—Juvenile
literature. [1. Alphabet.] I. Title.

    PE1155.B74 2001
    428.1—dc21
    [E]   00-42151

PRINTED AND BOUND IN BELGIUM

 Harry N. Abrams, Inc.
100 Fifth Avenue
New York, N.Y. 10011
www.abramsbooks.com

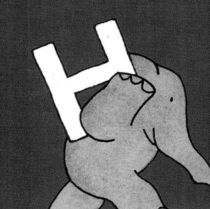